Trisha grew up in Surrey and spent a lot of her youth writing. Her first poem, *Granada,* which she wrote aged 12, is included in this book.

Trisha enjoys walking, reading and writing among her many hobbies.

Trisha now lives in West Sussex with her husband, Alex.

I dedicate this book to my parents, Henry and Vera, for their belief in me and to my family and friends for putting up with my poetry recitals over the years.

Trisha Alexander

TRISHA'S BOOK OF FUNNY AND AMUSING POEMS

AUSTIN MACAULEY PUBLISHERS™
LONDON • CAMBRIDGE • NEW YORK • SHARJAH

A CIP catalogue record for this title is available from the British Library.

ISBN 9781035838011 (Paperback)
ISBN 9781035838028 (ePub e-book)

www.austinmacauley.co.uk

First Published 2024
Austin Macauley Publishers Ltd®
1 Canada Square
Canary Wharf
London
E14 5AA

I would like to thank my husband, Alex, for his support over the years and to Austin Macauley for publishing my book.

Grotty Boys

Here we go – in a row, little boys without their toys.
Cos here's a sneeze and grubby knees.
With snotty nose plus scruffy toes,

On their shoes – who else would choose to be like this, for
them it's bliss.
Socks that pong – a dinner gong
Is a summons to eat that special treat.
Like a row round a lake, munching chocolate and cake.

With a toothy grin that your heart would win.
Yes, it would melt because you felt that your precious lad,
Acts just like his dad!

Henty

Henty was a chicken destined for the pot, the moment she
got wind of this
She thought that I will not
grace the dinner table as the mains before the pud
That's me out of here, whilst the goings good
She waited until nightfall before she fled the coop, noting
that the other hens were dozing in a group
They didn't seem to notice her as she pecked around the lock
or hear the chimes from the local church pealing midnight
on its clock
Suddenly, a shadow appeared on the path ahead
as Freddy Fox sniffed the air and then out loud,
he said, "Good evening, young lady, pray would you like a
date?"
"I know a romantic restaurant where they serve a juicy
steak"
He eyed her rump most eagerly as well as her plump breast
She took his arm smiled prettily and well, you can guess the
rest

Rufus

There was a dog called Rufus who used to drive a car
He didn't do it often nor did he drive far
He'd wear a scarlet baseball cap along with matching vest
Upon which "world's greatest dog" was emblazoned on his
chest
He'd sit upon his master's lap whilst steering with his paws
Of course, he couldn't wind down windows or open the car
door
But how he loved to toot the horn and wave to passers-by
As he watched them do a double take, and quickly rub their
eyes
They'd drive downtown for groceries and speak with Mr
Jones
Who often sold them tasty snacks and gave Rufus meaty
bones.
Whilst returning from a shopping trip one grey and rainy day
A policeman on his motorbike grimly blocked their way
He said dogs driving cars is strictly against the law
"May I see your licence please?" and Rufus held out a paw
He hadn't got a licence, he never took a test

So he gave the cop a knowing wink and pointed to his chest
At this, poor Rufus's master turned white and very pale
For now, they are both on holiday inside the county jail

Pants

My mother's Aunty Gertrude never wore her pants
Tho' she knew that it was risky, she clearly took that chance
For if out on a family picnic she went to spend a penny
She was always quickest cos she wasn't wearing any
One day in the depths of winter when deep snow lay on the ground
She went out all commando in the middle of the town
Alas, this luckless lady, 'twas hardly a surprise
caught a really dreadful chill, which led to her demise,
So always put your knickers on even if you're running late
lest with one chilblain too many
you share a similar fate

Lacy Tracy

Tracey's dress was lacy and her socks had girly frills
Her family delighted in playing with her in the surrounding
farmland hills
They often shared a picnic or lay warming themselves in the
sun
Which was a perfect way to spend a day enjoying a happy
time and family fun
Grandad Terry and Uncle Ryan often carried her shoulder
high
Whilst she shrieked with delight and pretended fright, gazing
up at the bright blue sky
They often wished they had a dog, but had a bunny instead,
which Tracy loved
And hugged goodnight before she went to bed
So, bless this special family and keep them safe and well
May their joys grow ever stronger with many more tales to
tell

The Journey

On a bus to Chichester, a note was passed along saying,
Hello, my name is John and though I am an ugly duckling,
pray will you be my swan?
If you accept this offer, please come and share my seat
And I'll open a pack of truffles we can share as a special
treat
I'll even take you out for tea and treat you like a queen
Who knows what romance we may conjure up, we might yet
discover love's dream
So come and be that special one, the one who can light my
fire
The one who can ride on the bus with me and of it never tire
He sat there waiting expectantly a smile upon his face
Hoping a pair of eager arms would reach out in a wild
embrace
Alas, his dream was shattered and the smile wiped off his
face
As an over-ample bottom plonked down in the empty space
He hadn't made a plan for this as a rather breathy man
Whispered "Hi there, handsome, I'd like to be your fan."
He's given up the buses our over ardent swain
He thinks that in future he'd rather take the train

Humpty Dumpty

Humpty Dumpty climbed a wall, which wasn't hard cos he
was tall
All the kings' horses and all the kings' men went to tea with
him now and then
Each of them wearing a smart red hat which they all
removed when they entered his flat
They slurped his tea and they scoffed his cakes, his scones,
his flapjacks and homemade bakes
Like all good guests, they washed their plates
Then spruced themselves up to go out on hot dates, they
romanced the ladies
They flirted like mad, looking and hoping for a chance to be
bad
For all boys are naughty if given the chance, eyeing the
girlies with a wink and a glance
Oh, the temptation and fun of it all just because Humpty
climbed the wall

The Guilty Gull

A gull went splat on a witch's hat, about which she was not
best pleased
Hence, tho' she wished for revenge
Her pride to avenge – she set free her rant as she started to
chant
"May your feathers turn blue with waterproof glue – may
you stick to a tree and never be free, till a maid comes along
with an exquisite song that makes your heart melt with love
that you never knew that you felt, thus with your tears,
finally free, you can no longer be imprisoned by me."

Clarissa

Clarissa was a pygmy goat who loved to swim to stay afloat,
She sported goggles and froggy flippers, kicking her hooves
like rampant kippers
Every day she practised her skill, training her hooves to
respond to her will
In no time at all, she won a gold medal, staying focused on
the progress pedal
Feeling proud of herself, her heart swelled with pride,
knowing the public were all on her side
So let's praise Clarissa for all her endeavours, as the rest of
us out there think she's been exceptionally clever

Wonky

Wonky was a worm who lived in a curled-up leaf and tho'
he munched on insect treats,
What he secretly wanted most was to own a gleaming set of
teeth,
He longed to bite into sausages and lamb with tangy mint
sauce,
He also fancied rare roast beef served with Yorkshire pud of
course.
So off he went to the dentist who sorted his gnashers out and
the moment he caught sight of these he gave a triumphant
shout,
"Look at me with my diamond teeth, gleaming in the sun,
shining bright like the stars at night.
Oh, how I love each and every one!"
He went back to hug the dentist and to thank him for his
smile, promising to brush most carefully
Whilst his teeth were put on trial.
Wonky grinned to himself for the rest of the day and smiled
as he looked into the glass,
Knowing that the days of having ugly teeth now lay in the
past.

Jake

There was a snake whose name was Jake
And who liked to squeeze people very tight and give them
all a nasty fright
Until one day, a man called Jim sought to take revenge on
him
By pouring neat vodka on his head
And now guess what? That snake is dead

Fran's Car

There was a car nicknamed knickers, that was owned by a
lady called Fran
Who broke down by a garage in Portsmouth where the
mechanics worked out a plan.
They eagerly scanned under the bonnet and bashed a few
nuts on the head, they were eager to please as they fell to
their knees scoffing sarnies from under the trees.
These guys were full of endeavour and meaning.
Alan, James and Liam, who worked thru the night vowing to
get it right in case our friend Fran tried to sue'em,
She wouldn't, of course, as we know and they put on a really
good show,
So well done to them, these genuine men, whom their
friends are all proud to know.

Our Emerald Anniversary

Fifty-five years together sounds a lot to me
I wonder if it does to the rest of you who are out there fancy
free
I can't say I envy you, for it's pure delight to share
Hugs and kisses with that special one with whom others
can't compare

Let's hold hands and bless our day
Allowing the rest of the world to hear us say
How lucky we are to enjoy wedded bliss
For no other couple could be as happy as this

Alinka

Alinka was a little boy to whom the angels gave a gift
This was at his christening and his special gift was this
They gave to him a magic branch made of burnished gold
upon which were woven leaves shining bright and bold
These leaves possessed a talent that he could give away
Such as manifesting a piano that one of his friends could
play
In time, his friend grew famous and played in concerts
around the world
He even played before the queen as a union jack unfurled
The second leaf he gifted was to a crippled little girl
she tried to walk without success until a leaf upon her dress
Worked its magic without delay till joyfully she skipped
away
A beaming smile upon her face and many hearts lifted in joy
All because of this special boy.
So trust that joy can be yours too
Which sometimes can be hard to do

Property Marcus

Marcus Mouse built a house up in the Hollywood hills
He liked it a lot with its extra-large plot
And its ornate wrought iron sills
His next-door neighbour named Kim often popped round for
a swim
And if she stayed for dinner, he was on to a winner
As she spent the night there with him
Thus, our Marcus enjoyed a nice life unencumbered by such
things as a wife
So he felt free to roam and bring buddies home without
causing upset or strife
No wonder he became a big star, admired by those near and
far
Directors implored him, leading ladies adored him
Begging to work with him
Going down on their knees, no wonder he became a
BIG CHEESE

Porkies

Hurrah for pigs of every size, out in fields or in their stys
Not on spits and never in sauce, I prefer them running
around of course
Their shiny snouts and trotty feet are meaty morsels I would
not eat
And pigs in blankets are not exempt, for my appetite they
could not tempt
So, celebrate our friendly pig, small or large or just plain big
Do not eat him if you please
Chomp instead your spuds and peas

The Tale of Stinky Greene

Stinky Greene was always seen with grubby hands and dirty
face
You couldn't take him any place
When he walked past all eyes were raised
For Stinky hadn't washed for days

Would you believe when he was near
Dogs would whine and cock an ear
There was no doubt it made folks gag
To see this walking garbage bag

Until one day it did transpire,
that Stinky's truck caught on fire
Five enormous hoses arrived with the fire crew
Without delay, they sprayed away at the truck and Stinky too

T'was quite a sight, this vivid scene
For Stinky Greene was squeaky clean

Sunday

"Please help me dry the dishes dear," his belittled woman
calls
Oh, blast he thinks unto himself, oh cricket bats and balls
"It will only take a minute dear," she cajolingly drones on
As he questions how he manages to get so put upon

Alright, so he has dried the lot, they are neatly stacked away
He thinks he'll read his newspaper, then he hears her say,
"The kitchen shelf you said you'll mend, it's rather urgent
pet,
And the invitation to the Wilsons, you haven't rung them
yet!"

He'd done all that she asked him, his expressions rather
glum
For he's wielded phone and hammer and chiselled on his
thumb
A voice floats out from the kitchen, "Please, darling, don't
forget
that mothers coming round for lunch and the table isn't set."

And on the seventh day he rested, what a caustic rub
He's slaving when he should be swigging whisky in the pub
He thinks of Belle the barmaid, a sigh escapes his lips
Oh, her over-ample bosom and her generous curving hips

"It's time to carve the roast dear, lunch is ready John."
'Tis not till some hours later, she sees his clothes have gone

The Hangover

His face is looking really green, the greenest face he's ever
seen
He prays he's having some ghoulish dream
About the demon alcohol
As hand on the basin edge, he props, way down on the
bathroom floor he flops
He swears he'll never touch a drop
Another drop of alcohol
Oh, burning brow and fever lips, why did he think he'd get
his kicks
To place himself in such a fix
Through that infernal alcohol
The ceilings spinning, so is the floor and in his ears a
thunderous roar
He's suffering from the night before
And that seductive alcohol
Oh, what an ass, a fool he's been. He doesn't think drinking
is his scene
Next time he'll not be quite so keen
To join his friends in alcohol
As with them, he launched forth to sup, they said he's got
some catching up

To do, and so he stood his ground and manfully he paid his round
For that liquid poison alcohol
Oh lord, he's feeling really bad, he's lost count of the drinks he's had
His girlfriend's going to be quite mad
As she sees the effect of alcohol
Her lover solely clad in a gown, will get a real dressing down
Unitedly they'll sternly frown
Upon that fiendish alcohol
She seems far madder than he thought, so now he wonders, if he ought
To offer refreshments of some sort, perhaps a little glass of port
A cheering glass of alcohol?

The Victorious Matador

A rounded disc so void and empty

stared at by a thronging crowd
heralds oft a flaming figure
blessed and admired by voices loud

Hark at his swirling cloak of crimson
Yellow and bloodied as a fire
hear again the shouting figures
that this cruelty never tires

Hail this dance of mounting passion
Scent the murder in the air
Feel a pity over victory
And for the conquered one, despair

As on the ground there lies depression
Nowhere are there mourners near
Only the empty sky observes
The real hero, is not here

Santa's Lesson

When Santa came down the chimney at speed, his reindeer
were in a hurry to feed
On the many peeled carrots in place, with Mr Claus anxious
to taste
The generous glass of vintage wine and the mature stilton
with its flavour divine

After several mince pies, Santa sat down for a rest
Discovering that his appetite had put him to the test
For very soon, he fell asleep and then began to snore
Until a dozen heads appeared from around the kitchen door

Oh, what a horrid shock he had, to see the family's Mum
and Dad
As well as their daughters and little lad
This made him feel so very bad

For the first time ever, he'd let a family down
Imagine what the world would say
Why, they'd probably run him out of town!
But wait a minute, all's not lost
There was a reason that their paths had crossed

For they were meant to share their joy, with every other girl
and boy
Rejoice and be glad, please don't be sad, for
Christmas day is really here and
All is well with nowt to fear.

Magic

Mud pies, sparkling eyes, smiling faces, untied laces.
The magic of childhood knows no bounds.
From belief in fairies to wizards and clowns, pixies and
goblins and gossamer wings
Birdsong at bedtime, in castles by kings
Spider spun webs by day and by night, witch chanted spells
putting all wrongs to right
Wave badness away and bring forth the light.
Slumber safely and sweetly throughout the night, hugs and
kisses from Angels
Keep you all safe and warm, protected and cosy, enfolded
till dawn.

Malti

Malti stuck his head out from underneath his shell
Thoughtfully, he sniffed the air as his lungs began to swell
He caught the scent of lettuce leaves and of cabbage leaves
as well
Trying hard to build his dream of where pride in himself
should dwell
He was desperate to become a movie star or a personality of
note
A sportsman or an artist of whom everybody spoke
He didn't want to be James Bond, no, he never fancied that
yet.
Suddenly, it dawned on him, he'd love to be a vet
So off he went to college, his rucksack on his back
Containing notepad, pen and paper
And the veterinary college map
He attended many lectures where he learned about potions
and pills
Bandaging and sutures, anaesthetics and of drills
This was highly skilful work where wisdom filled his head
Leading to the expertise that would stand him in good stead

He is now a global professor, a true master of his art, and
A close buddy of Professor Fitzpatrick whom you could also rival
Should you choose to work as hard

Christmas Surprise

Hello Santa. Hello Elves
Never thought I'd see you here, busy stacking shelves
Fancy you working at Tesco's, I'm guessing times are hard
What with feeding all those reindeer, and those toys you've
got to guard
Where's your sleigh and where's your sack, I suppose
you've hidden them round the back.
Take care the boss doesn't see them, otherwise, you'll get
the sack

I think you'd better get going as time is marching on and
letting the world's kiddies down
Simply isn't on
So, here's a couple of mince pies and here's a cup of tea
Thanks a lot, old Santa,
In the morning, I'll look under my tree

Soul Song

Akashic records, a bygone age shows karmic lives on every
page
Silken threads weave their veil, as each one spins its magic
tale
Delicate as butterfly wings, a golden song to each soul sings
A heart already spoken for on an ordinary day
Suddenly, a certain face halts it on its way
A hint of recognition of a life lived long ago
No inkling of the karma to stem its ebb and flow
No arrows pointing forward, to show the road ahead
Somehow, it feels like last time when words were left unsaid
An hourglass so fragile snatched a life away
Knowing through the sands of time, you'd be missed every
day
Lashes damp with teardrops misted in the past
The precious moments from the now, ever holding its love
fast
Once it is ignited the flame of love burns on
Wearing many guises till it sings its final song

New Year Wishes

I wish you a happy new year with many months of joy
And if you are looking, may romance find you that special
girl or boy
May the church bells echo with every happy sound
Ringing out around you, may your feet not touch the ground
May love and hugs be everywhere
May your arms catch everyone
with every shadow swept away in an avalanche of fun
let's gather in the new year with love and hugs galore
may the affection of that special one be with you evermore

Seasons

Don't dip your toe in the water yet Matilda,
It really is much too cold
An arctic wind blew yesterday, so in the snowflakes rolled
They blew upon the hedgerows and all around the lake
Glistening in the sunshine like icing on a cake
Children were out there sledging
smiling and having fun
Throwing snowballs at each other
whilst Dad held hands with Mum
Although the date was the 3rd of May,
And summer should be here
Mother nature needs fun too
Regardless of the time of year

Percy's Song

Half a dozen Percy's standing in a row
Went for a walk across the park, when it began to snow
As the snowflakes got much bigger
They began to lose their way
For the snowflakes covered their paw marks and the
youngest started to say
"I think I want my mummy cos it's dark and I'm scared."
Then a voice boomed out of nowhere
"Even if you cannot see me, you need to know I'm always
there
For I'm your guardian angel and I've been with you since
you were born
So, dry those little tear drops and my wings will keep you
warm
For I'll make sure you're safe
So don't be frightened any more, as all you need is faith."

Olly

Olly sat forlornly beside the garden gate
Gazing into the distance above his dinner plate
He was feeling hungry tho', dinnertime was more than past
And usually, his dinner was a much-enjoyed repast

Something was upsetting him and had been so for days
Nobody could quite tell why unless it was just a phase
Yogi, Olly's owner, studied his doggie's face
Searching for some hint or clue to which this misery
Could be traced
A moment of enlightenment flitted across Yogi's eyes
As gradually it dawned on him the obvious reason why
His much-loved doggie, Olly, had forgotten something of
import
And that was how to wag his tail, his reason for feeling
distraught
Yogi gave Olly a hug and he began to wag his tail
Once started he couldn't stop, thus happiness did prevail

Granada

Praise be for the beauties of Granada
From the dreaming of Vega and the Alhambra
The soft guitar dripping pearls of sound
As swarthy Gitanos to its rhythms pound
Saffron her roofs, exquisite her chiming bells
Haunting gardens wherein a breathless current swells
Fragrant Bougainvillaea, a screen of colour splayed.
Purple sierras 'neath citadels of ragged Jade
Siesta hour when all the earth is still
And the scorching sun, a drugging pill
Weeping stars steeped in the virginal dusk
Throw forth their tears to the thirsty dust
This tragic beauty, a veil of endless sighs
Is a prayer unsaid to the brooding skies

Your Best Friend

Let us salute man's best friend.
For your home, he'll guard and your flocks he'll tend
He'll carry your paper, then bring you your slippers.
If your busy with laundry, he'll abscond with your knickers.

He'll beat you at football and chew the plants by your door.
If you spill morning cornflakes, he'll lick clean your floor.

He'll put his nose in your dinner, then sniff his bum.
Wagging his tail finding his life joyously great fun.

You know that you love him and that he loves you too.
And that he'll always be faithful in whatever you do.